D1559046

Stretch Your Mind

Adopt a Growth Mindset, Generate Unique Ideas, Create Unbelievable Opportunities, and Live Life on Your Terms.

By Zoe McKey

zoemckey@gmail.com

www.zoemckey.com

Table Of Contents

Introduction

In 2019 I read 85 books.

I'm not telling you this to brag or make you feel bad about how many books you read last year. I think before then—not including the *Harry Potter* series—I hadn't read 85 books myself, in all my life.

But in 2019 I was in a hard place, and I desperately needed wisdom. People say, find someone in your environment who lives the way you'd like to live and just do what they do. But what if there's no such person around you? What if you're constantly on the road and you can't establish deep relationships? What if your geography, job, or financial means limit you and prevent you from being around such people?

Not all of us are blessed with a flesh-and-bone mentor walking beside us, holding our hands. What can we do? Give up? Accept that life didn't deal us those cards and numb our pain with something? Most people certainly do that. They decide their life problems can't be fixed, so they start avoiding the pain of this notion with a substance, an activity—or inactivity.

"Are you one of those people?" I asked myself when life kicked me to my emotional and physical rock bottom.

I wish I could tell you that I heroically screamed "NO!" and rose from the ground on an energy-filled, stormy cloud, and went the distance unwaveringly while lightning and thunder powered the hefty beat of my heart and stallions ran beside me as I completed my mission and fulfilled my destiny.

Nope. My answer to this question was something much more serene and insecure. I didn't know how to answer this question. I didn't know if I was a quitter, someone who was predestined to be how she was, who could never leave her mental limitations and blocks behind. There were no clouds and stallions, just my silent sobbing echoing in an empty room in Taipei, Taiwan, in the house of someone who loved and hated me at the same time. I felt so alone. I knew no one in that town whom I wanted to resemble. I had no friends or family nearby.

All I had was one book that I bought a few weeks ago at a second-hand shop, and I only got it because, frankly, it was the only one whose title I could decipher. (I don't speak or read Mandarin.) It was Brene Brown's *Rising Strong*.

"I don't believe in supernatural powers." And whenever I am cocky enough to state this, life throws something in front of me amusedly saying,

"Oh, really?" Randomly stumbling onto a book called *Rising Strong* when you feel you are weak and have hit rock bottom... Let's just say the Universe has a weird sense of humor.

I still remember picking up that book and starting to flip through its pages... Do you know that scene in *Harry Potter* when Harry finds the Pensieve in Dumbledore's room and falls into it and sees the memories of the headmaster? That's how I felt reading Brown's book. Getting to know her a little bit more through her work. Being able to detach from my story, and immerse myself in someone else's. Learning about pain and joy; failures and successes; words of wisdom learned the hard way.

Suddenly it occurred to me. I don't need anyone around me to change myself for the better, to learn, and to gain the wisdom I was so thirsty for. I have literally everything I need at my fingertips. Books.

I could have Ray Dalio as a mentor. Or Abraham Lincoln. Or Jane Austen. Heck, I could even have Amy Poehler!

And I had them all. As I told you, I read 85 books in 2019. Because I needed them. Because I wanted to learn, to know more, to grow better. Because when we recycle the information in our head over and over, we won't get ahead. We'll just get whiplash from spinning so much.

No one needs to be "that person," it turns out, who has no other choice but to resign to life's unchangeable nature. Books hold all the knowledge anyone needs to thrive. And books are available—from Goodwill to libraries, from Amazon to Barnes and Noble, you can find them. Or as you can see in my case, they can find you.

This book isn't about my thoughts, but the thoughts others inspired me to think. This book doesn't summarize my best practices, but the practices the best use that made me become better. The aim of *The Unlimited Mind* is to give you a glimpse into the unlimited collective mind of humanity in which you can tap into any time you want. This book is a compilation of my favorite reads, the lessons I learned from them, and tips on how to use these lessons to your own benefit.

Chapter 1: On Resistance

"More gold has been mined from the thoughts of men than has been taken from the earth. So dust off the cobwebs and use all those great ideas you have!"

— Unknown Author

Did you ever daydream of the person you might become? Do you have an idea of who you are meant to be? Are you passionate about something that you would like to accomplish?

But at the same time, do you also tell yourself that your vision is impossible to turn into reality? Are you an entrepreneur in your dreams, but have never started a business? Are you an artist—a painter, let's say—who's never touched a canvas with a brush?

If you identified with this description, you're not alone. I dare say, all of us face this problem in our life quite often. We have a vision but something intangible stops us from taking action.

In one of my "mentor's," Steven Pressfield's, words, we live in *resistance*.

Pressfield, the author of *The War of Art*, highlights that as rational and rationalizing beings, in the first round we identify resistance coming from outside of us. It's not us, but our partner, our parents, environment, bad education, lousy job, the boss, late public transportation. They are responsible for our delayed dreams—not us. We always find a reason why not to do what we wish.[i]

The truth is, fulfilling our dreams is our responsibility. Every time we are discouraged or talked out of our true desires, it's because we've allowed it.

Resistance always arises from within. People generate and maintain it. It's not about the wall that gets erected in front of you, it's about your reaction to it. Do you stop or do you try to climb it?

Resistance is directly proportional to the importance of our desires. The more we long for something, the more resistance we'll feel to actually starting it. It's not that we don't want to do it. Usually, the subject of our resistance is all we want! Just, the time is not right now. We need more knowledge, free time, or money to start it. We rationalize and justify why we shouldn't do our work.[ii]

Dreaming about our dreams feels extraordinary, but delaying the achievement due to resistance feels horrible. In Dreamland, we feel good, but as soon as we switch back to reality and start thinking about the execution, we don't feel like taking action. We're bored and restless at the same time.

Some become so comfortable in their resistance that they convince themselves they aren't good at anything; they aren't talented, don't have ideas, or aren't worthy of a better life. The reality is that they have ideas but resist trying them out because they don't have positive feedback from previous successes.

Why? Most likely because they didn't try to do something that defines them, something they wanted for themselves before.

I won't sell you snake oil; we are not born with unlimited choices. We can't be anything we want to be. For example, I'd love to be an acknowledged singer, but unless I perform for a deaf audience, I have zero chances of accomplishing it. And that's okay.

Our task on this planet Earth is not to constantly fight against who we are; disliking what we got, and wishing for something else, but to find and accept who we are and make the most of what we have.

"Everyone is gifted—but some people never open their package!"
— Wolfgang Riebe

You may never become a world-class performer or athlete. Maybe you don't aim for these titles. But you can always become your best self. You can always work hard to be the best you. This is true personal excellence.

Harnessing from your best self you can find a couple of traits which combine uniquely in you, make you special in your own way, and provide value to the world. Find these traits and capitalize on them—financially, emotionally, and spiritually.

For example, I have a way of deeply understanding my own and other people's emotions. In other words, I have good interpersonal and intrapersonal skills. But I only discovered this recently. Before, I attributed my success to luck. Having a good conversation or preventing a fight from happening by using the right emotional tools just seemed like something happening by chance. Until they happened so often and in so many different situations that I had to acknowledge the only common factor in all these equations was me.

What was the "luck" and "chance" story, then? That, my friends, was resistance. I always dreamed of being an empathetic, kind, and socially responsible person. But how could the daughter of a cheerful narcissist and a warm-hearted schizophrenic, someone who used to steal and lie to stay afloat in her teenage years, be a good and compassionate being? On some level I was afraid of becoming the person I wished to be because of my past and lack of examples. Even if evidence was showing me what I was good at, I resisted.

What would it mean if I accepted that I was good and kind and loving? Well, first of all, I'd lose the identity my false self created to protect me from my mother's absence and my father's emotionally hurtful ways of relating. I ignore the pain of not having my mom around mentally, because I'm bad and uncaring. It makes sense. I morph into what my father wants me to be so I can get his attention because I'm bad and sneaky. It makes sense, too. This story made sense to me at the time and helped me survive my teenage years as an emotional clam. But my true nature showed through the mask over and over again.

Do you know how my resistance disappeared about acknowledging my inner goodness? By embracing that I am good *because* of the mask. The pain behind the mask is what forged me into the person I am today. The light I feel that floods my body and soul infiltrated through the little cracks of the mask at a special angle. I understand human emotions and pain well because I went through a lot of emotional pain myself. I saw firsthand human suffering through the destiny of my mother and suffered for being oblivious through the destiny of my father.

"The greatest thing a man can do in this world is to make the most possible out of the stuff that has been given him. This is success, and there is no other."
— Orison Swett Marden

Getting to know the best parts of you to discover your "personal excellence" is not the end of the road; it's only the beginning. If you have your unique essence, the real work is just about to begin. It's a lifetime of consistent and diligent improvement of this skill mix. Unless you were born as a genius in something, your "personal excellence" is still far from being good enough. You have to work on it.

Focus on your skill and the path you chose. You might not be passionate about it in the beginning. There is no rule that what we're good at and choose to do will be loved from the first instance. As Carl Newport says in his book *So Good They Can't Ignore You*, if you steadfastly and unwaveringly improve yourself in your work, you'll end up loving it and develop passion for it.[iii] "Move your focus away from finding the right work, toward working right, and eventually build a love for what you do." As Ralph Waldo Emerson said, "The successful man is the average man, focused."

Regardless if this "work" is sculpting your best self, becoming the best pickle maker, or the inventor of flying cars, it will need your work and dedication.

Why Should You Aim to Become a Professional Instead of an Amateur? (Apart From the Obvious Reasons.)

Aim to become a pro instead of an amateur. Amateur, as a word, originates from the root meaning "to love." This leads to the conventional interpretation that amateurs love what they do and pursue it, driven by the emotion of love. On the other hand, professionals do their job for money. In Steven Pressfield's opinion, amateurs don't love the game. If they did, they would make their calling their real vocation. Amateurism implies a way of laziness in this interpretation: they don't love what they do badly enough to dedicate their lives to it. There's a lack of full-time commitment in amateurs.[iv]

The professional mindset is open to challenges. They stretch their limits. That's what helps them grow. They also embrace fear. If they feel petrified in front of a challenge, it is a good sign. It means there is the possibility for improvement because the solution is not up their sleeve. Fear shows the way to gaining greater knowledge. "Success comes from continually expanding your frontiers in every direction—creatively, financially, spiritually, and physically. Always ask yourself, what can I improve? Who else can I talk to? Where else can I look?"[v]

Professionals not only recognize the growing possibilities, but also their limits. They know they are professionals in their "personal excellence" only. Therefore, they hire other professionals around themselves like lawyers, accountants, and designers.

Professionals love their work in the real sense. They accept money as the reward of hard work. If professionals didn't love what they did, they wouldn't devote their lives to it.

How Do You Stop Resistance in Your Life and Start Doing What You're Delaying?

"How things look on the outside of us depends on how things are on the inside of us."

— Parks Cousins

Stop for a moment and look around yourself. Do you like what you see? Now, look inside yourself. Do you feel satisfied? Is something bothering you? What triggers your resistance? If you want to make a change and get out of the rut, take a hard look at your life-to-date thoughts and choices. You can't achieve a different outcome with the same mentality.

If you feel that you were in resistance until now, and you repressed your personal excellence, it's time to change.

You have to consider yourself worthy of your dreams.

Because you are. It doesn't matter what you did in the past; you can't change it. The best you can do about your past is to harness the lessons it taught you, and move on. Make a mental note about your mistakes, strive to not commit them again, and move on. Forgive yourself and start writing a different future.

Exercises for This Chapter:

1. Today, I identified my personal excellence:

_____

2. Today, I identified the false stories I tell myself that prevent me from evolving my personal excellence:

1, 2, 3, 4…
_____

3. Today, I questioned and eliminated this false story:

For example: Today, I decided I can be a good public speaker even if I messed up the spelling contest in elementary school. I prepaid for a course to improve my communication skills...

Chapter 2: On Opportunities

"Did you know that opportunities are never lost? Someone will always take the ones you miss!"
— Unknown Author

Some people seemingly have so many opportunities to improve their lives. Others feel they haven't got any. Some say opportunities are the result of being in the right place at the right time. Others believe that, to have opportunities, one has to create them.

I think that the truth lies in the middle. While conscious and mindful planning and preparing increases the chance to get opportunities one hopes for, luck (being at the right place at the right time) is also needed for an amazing opportunity. I'd say a good opportunity equals knowledge plus hard work and some luck; an outstanding opportunity equals more knowledge plus harder work and a lot of luck.

If I add talent into any part of this equation, the opportunity's quality instantly bumps up a level. Namely, knowledge and hard work, a little luck, and talent create an outstanding opportunity. More knowledge and harder work, a lot of luck, and talent creates those one-in-a-million chances that all those people got whose names we know today—top performers, actors, politicians, and so on.

Two of these variables are controllable: the knowledge and hard work. They depend on you. If you work hard and gather knowledge diligently, but you don't particularly excel at anything, you can still create better opportunities for yourself than those who only sit and wait for a miracle.

The other two variables, luck and talent, however, are out of your control. Maybe you're born with a talent, maybe you're not. And you certainly can't influence luck. Being born with an outstanding talent is something that can be considered luck as well. However, talent by itself has never created opportunities.

You can be the most gifted singer on the planet, but if you were born in Bangladesh and only learned how to sew, you'll end up in a garment factory for forty cents an hour. It is still a better fate than being in the mines. If you can work hard on your singing skills and become the best singer in the area, your reputation might open some small doors, like becoming a singer in a fancier hotel or bar in Bangladesh, but that's the most you can expect to get out of hard work, knowledge, and talent. If someone important in show business happens to hear you in the hotel or bar, they may give you a chance to release an album and become the next hot thing in Bangladesh. This is the pure luck factor. However, the luck was partially due to your hard work. I mean, the show business guru wouldn't have discovered you humming in the garment factory, right?

Luck is a very complex variable. Many factors determine it, as we saw in the example of the singer above. If you were born to a rich family with great connections, you're talented, you have a good work ethic, and you had a singer as a father, you're suddenly Enrique Iglesias! But this situation is very rare.

A regular person's best chance to encounter good or outstanding opportunities is to create the necessary "infrastructure" for them. In other words, be knowledgeable and work as hard as possible on developing your skills, making connections, becoming presentable, whatever you need for your dream, so that when luck and opportunity finally find you, you're as ready as possible. (We're never quite ready to jump into something, don't forget that.)

Opportunity may knock on your door only once while temptation and distractions lay on the doorbell all day. Don't cease learning and working hard just because you haven't seen a good opportunity yet. Sometimes the opportunities are disguised. They are rarely a direct email from a company like General Electric for a CEO position.

Opportunities, more often than not, are good ideas that run through our minds, or ideas we run across, while we learn.

For example, I wasn't ready to become an English self-help writer the first time this opportunity came up. But I learned English well, I did my due diligence about human psychology, and I developed a curious, open mind. So I wasn't ready, per se, but I was as ready as possible to embrace the opportunity and work with it. Had I instead gotten an opportunity to work for SpaceX, I probably would have passed on it. My only redeeming knowledge there would have been my ability to read.

The Idea Machine Method

Good opportunities don't have to be external. They can be the result of some good ideas we create.

How do you generate good ideas?

James Altucher, another mentor of mine, presents a complex study of how to become an *idea machine* in his book *Choose Yourself*.

"Write down 10 ideas each day,"[vi] he says. So simple, right? In theory, everybody could do this. But not many of us do it. Why? Because of resistance. Because writing down 10 ideas daily is difficult, even if you can write about anything you want. Even the improvement of a stick bug colony's procreation. Thinking about three ideas is not challenging. Even five ideas can come together

34

with minor effort. To conceive 10 new ideas daily is not a piece of cake. Your brain needs to sweat. It has to step out of the box into the field of the extraordinary.

Not every idea will be good, though. What's more, Altucher says that 99% of our ideas will be rubbish. Still, our brain will be conditioned to constantly function to create. As a result, we'll have that 1% of good ideas that will eventually create opportunities for us.

How Do You Increase the Chances of Having Good Ideas?

Read for at least an hour a day. Divide this time to read about at least four different topics. Yesterday I read an article on the 2020 Iowa caucus, a chapter from a book called *If Buddha Ever Dated*, one chapter from *Where the Crawdads Sing*, and the rest of the time I spent on fishing for ideas in

The Millionaire Next Door. They are different topics, and not all of them add to the improvement of my main skills, but they expand my overall knowledge and perspective on the world.

Write down your 10 ideas on a daily basis. These can be business ideas, book ideas, ideas for surprising your spouse or parents, ideas for what you should do if you lose your leg, ideas for how to change your bed sheets quicker, whatever you can think of. The only rule is that it has to be at least 10 ideas on paper.

If you are persistent, by the end of a year, you will have read for almost one thousand hours and written down 3,650 ideas. If the calculation is true, you'll have at least 36 good ideas for the year. That's three good ideas a month. Depending on the time and energy demands of the idea's implementation, you might not even be able to do this amount of ideas justice.

Altucher estimates that to become an idea machine, it takes at least six months of daily practice. The idea muscle has to be exercised every day, otherwise it weakens like any other muscle. For example, if you skip the gym for two weeks, even if you are a high-performance athlete, you'll feel the difference. Your idea muscle will feel it, too.

Don't Look Back in Anger on Failure. It Can Be an Opportunity.

"Opportunities are found by those who look for them. The bee has a sting but honey too... so look at every negative and make a positive out of it."
— Unknown Author

Every failure we face is an opportunity in disguise: a chance to learn, to improve ourselves, to get to know our limits, to gain experience. Your life is mostly defined by the reactions you have to certain events. If you choose to look at failures or lost opportunities as lessons, you'll grow as a person. If you choose to lick your wounds and give up, you indeed lost.

We're human. We can't always say, "Okay, who cares? I'll take it as a lesson." We are emotional beings and failures are painful. Some more than others. There is nothing wrong with taking an emotional break to heal and revisit our lessons later.

Yet every tragedy has a mourning period after which the bad feelings slowly fade, unless we keep them alive artificially, getting stuck in the pits of complaining and self-victimization. If something hurts, cry it out—don't keep it in. But don't conflate a deep, loud scream with never-ending weeping.

Freedom Equals Opportunity.

What do you think about when you hear the words "good opportunity"? I usually associate them with advancements in a career, or financial gains. "I got a good opportunity to…" usually translates to "I got a job offer with good salary or good prospects."

The best opportunities that come in life are largely not about career or money. Quite the opposite—the best opportunities are those that grant more freedom. Work hard and gather knowledge on how to realize yourself without the need to be present in your work all the time. Strive to create the opportunity to do what you desire. There is a difference between having the opportunity of great work and having the opportunity to do whatever you want—and you may choose to work. But you don't need to. In my opinion, the opportunity of choice is very powerful.

How can one achieve this? Tim Ferriss, in his book *The 4-Hour Work Week*, talks about how to set up a business and a lifestyle which will learn to work by itself, requiring less and less of your physical and mental presence.

The best way is to "own the trains, and have someone else ensure they run on time." Strive to be the owner, not the boss; this way you'll have freedom and you can choose to work, too.

What Is the Correlation between Money and Freedom?

You have quite a few Ws in your life: what, when, where, and who. Your money gets multiplied in practical value, depending on how many Ws you control in your life:

- What do you want to do?
- When do you want to do it?
- Where do you want do it?
- Who do you want to do it with?[vii]

These are called the "freedom multipliers." How does this work in practice? A rich, but busy, employee making six figures per year, based on "freedom multipliers," has a weaker position than someone who makes only $50,000 by working from home a few hours per day and owns all his Ws.

Options are the real opportunities. That's where true power lies. How do you see and create those options with the least effort and cost?

First, don't stay idle for too long. It will poison your creative brain and willpower. Easy things quickly become habits, especially if practiced often. In this regard, it doesn't matter if you're generally optimistic and idle, or pessimistic and idle.

"There's no difference between a pessimist who says 'Oh, it's hopeless, don't bother doing anything.'—and an optimist who says 'Everything's

fine—don't bother doing anything.' Either way, nothing happens."

— Tim Ferriss

It may sound counterintuitive, but being busy is just as unhelpful as staying idle when you are reaching to gain freedom. Being busy is a synonym for avoiding the critical but uncomfortable tasks. Busyness is a form of laziness: "lazy thinking and indiscriminate action." Being overwhelmed is as unproductive as doing nothing, and far more unpleasant.

Let's face it, most of the time when we're busy, we really shouldn't be. We don't take the time to think about what to do and what doesn't matter. We just pick up the next task we see because it's easier. If we manage our time well, prioritizing the most important tasks and executing them on time, we wouldn't be overwhelmed.

Doing something unimportant well does not make it important. Time-consuming tasks won't become important just because they require a lot from your most precious asset.[viii]

What you do is much more important than *how* you do it. Finishing the tasks that matter in a mediocre manner is infinitely better than executing something unimportant perfectly. "Efficiency is useless unless applied to the right things." And with most tasks, it makes no difference.

Instead, be selective. Take the time and mental power to separate important tasks from time-stuffing ones. Do less. This is the way to productivity improvement. Set your mind on those few important things that deliver the most value (income, fame, help, love—whatever your goals would be) and ignore the rest. *Lack of time is a lack of priorities in disguise.*

The first focus optimization you can do is to improve your strengths instead of trying to fix your weaknesses. Taking your "personal excellence" to a professional level is much more important—and rewarding and fun—than to struggle to lift your weaknesses to a tolerable or mediocre level.

How Do You Distinguish Productive Tasks From the Unproductive Ones?

The first productivity indicator you can use to decide the usefulness of an action is the *Pareto Principle,* or the 80/20 Rule. What does this mean?

The principle states that 80% of effects flow from 20% of causes, or that 80% of results come from 20% of effort and time. In economics, as a rule of thumb, 80% of profits come from 20% of customers. This ratio is not set in stone, a 70%–30% or 90%–10% ratio can still be rooted in the Pareto Principle.[ix]

Based on the Pareto Principle, answer the following questions:

- Which 20% of actions help me finish 80% of my tasks?
- Which 20% of time intervals is my productivity zone, where I'm 80% more focused than other times?
- Which 20% of people and activities are causing 80% of my problems and unhappiness?
- Which 20% of people and activities are resulting in 80% of my desired outcomes and happiness?

The second productivity indicator is Parkinson's Law. The official definition for it is the following:

"Work expands so as to fill the time available for its completion." In other words, if you allow yourself one week to complete a task, that's how long is going to take. If you allow yourself a month, that's how long the same task's completion will take.

There is magic in imminent deadlines. If you give yourself only a day to complete a project, the pressure of time scarcity will force you to focus on what matters about the execution. You literally won't have time to actively procrastinate.

Try out this method. Pick a task and give yourself 24 hours to complete it. Be strict about it and don't cheat. Consider this task a life-or-death project. While executing it, take notes on your focus points, which activities helped you the most in completion, when you were the most creative, and so forth. Making a trial task like this can help you get valuable information about how well you manage your time, if your prioritization is adequate, and so on.

How do you work under pressure? What are your strengths? What helps you, what distracts you?

Doing this exercise more and more often will help you develop the habit of how to work quickly and efficiently on a short deadline. You will gather valuable information about yourself and you'll know where you need to improve.

Studies showed that those who got one month to execute a task and those who got only two days had almost the same results. The work of those who had less time was more solution oriented. Because of the time scarcity, they focused only on those parts that directly contributed to the task.

The Pareto Principle and Parkinson's Law can serve as a base to free your time, and create for yourself the opportunity of choice:

1. Limit your tasks to the important, to shorten your work time (Pareto Principle)

2. Shorten your work time to limit tasks to the important (Parkinson's Law)

Identify a couple of important tasks that add the most value to your goals, and schedule them with very short and clear deadlines.

Set Yourself Productivity Reminders to Check up on Yourself Every Day.

I have three alarms set (apart from my wake up and bedtime alarms) in my Alarm App on the phone. One at 10 a.m., one at 3 p.m., and one at 5 p.m., showing the same message: "Am I productive? Is it important what I'm doing now?" I recommend that you try it. Sometimes I'm guilty of wandering around on the Internet. When my phone pings at me with a crossed look, I feel like a child who just got caught lying, so I close my browsers and go back to work. Demonstrating results is much more important than just being active.

You can also set some time-saving rules for yourself. Direct all communication you have during the day toward immediate action. Limit reading and answering emails to once a day or once a week if you can. Set an auto responder saying you're only checking email once a day or week. Use www.rescuetime.com to see how much time you spend on different tasks, and block some distracting websites while you work.

If you work as an employee for a company, spending time on nonsense is sometimes not your fault. Unfortunately, most institutions don't incentivize workers to use time well—unless they are paid on commission. Working an hourly wage is the worst. This work style encourages workers to finish work in as much time as possible to get more payment for less effort. Time is wasted because there is so much time available. Even if you're employed, you don't have to waste time. Be smarter.

Finish your real job-related tasks as quickly and as well as possible, then put it to rest. Then, work and study on your own projects. As I mentioned in the previous chapter, knowledge and hard work always pay off. At the end of your work day, check again what you did for work in the morning, finalize it, and send it. (Unless you had a deadline to finish the task quicker.) This way, your workplace won't consider you useless; you did your job.

If, however, you feel that there's a chance to bargain for a flexible work schedule, or getting paid by results instead of time spent (wasted) in the office, go for that instead. Ask for more flexible hours, for working more from Monday to Thursday and then having Friday off every second week. There are options you can play with— sometimes all you need to do is ask. Do your job quickly and professionally, and then embrace your new free time to do something else.

If you get your free time, don't forget that you didn't make it happen just to become a couch potato. You got it to eventually liberate more Ws in your life.

Exercises for This Chapter:

1. My 10 ideas about anything today are:

      1,   2,   3,   ...   10

_____

2. Today's top three activities I can use to fill my free time to be productive are:

      1,   2,   3...

_____

3. If there was only one thing I could accomplish in my free time, it would be:

_____

Chapter 3: On Dreams

"Most things that we think are impossible in life is because we have never tried them. So go for every dream and opportunity before making a judgment."

— Unknown Author

I'm always amazed by how many different meanings some letter combinations can have. For example, if we look at the word "impossible," it has a negative connotation. It means something will never happen. If we look at the same 10 letters using some spaces and apostrophes, it can transform into "I'm possible," and it gets the opposite meaning.

It is just as simple to switch your mindset from "no" to "yes." Remember, success comes in cans, failure in can'ts.

It doesn't matter if you have a humble dream or an earth-shockingly big, ridiculous, and unbelievable one—there is no such thing as impossible. (Except my career as a singer.) If "impossible" truly existed, we wouldn't have people like Albert Einstein, Neil Armstrong, or Barack Obama. All of these people did something that decades and centuries before was considered to be impossible.

So who knows? Maybe you can achieve your wildest dreams. Maybe you won't. Maybe your timing was not the best. Or you didn't work hard enough. Or some bad luck was involved. Or you should have shown more flexibility with your goal's parameters… I don't want to sell you the idea that if you want to play Luke Skywalker in the next *Star Wars* installment, it's possible if you work hard enough while being, say, an Asian female. That goal just doesn't make sense. Although some people still try it.

Why am I even saying this? Because I'm projecting an old embarrassment into this reversed role-seeking scenario. I, Zoe McKey, a white-Caucasian female, at the age of 11, sent an email to Warner Bros. to consider me for the role of Cho Chang in the upcoming *Harry Potter* movies with the deliberate aim that I wanted to kiss Harry Potter (Daniel Radcliffe). Luckily, I can use my age as an excuse for that.

There is, however, a legend who still lives among us who proved that impossible is just an excuse not once, but three times. He got to the top of the three most-hyped career paths of the 20th and 21st century: athletics, acting, and politics. He did all this as a foreigner and a non-native English speaker (maybe that's why he's so inspiring to me) in a foreign country. This person is Arnold Schwarzenegger.

I recently read his book *Total Recall*. If you need an inspirational person who challenges you to think big, he is the right choice.

He is extraordinarily ambitious, and behind his ambitious words there are rock-solid achievements. Even those who don't like him because of his political opinion can agree that his bodybuilding and acting career achievements are admirable. (Except maybe some very bad movies like *Jingle All The Way*.) But all in all, he's a rock star. He is The American Dream!

When I feel blue and down, and everything seems so impossible, I take his book off the shelf, read a few pages, and like Popeye with his spinach, I get refueled by Arnold's optimism and get my ass to work.

If you don't know much about Arnold's past, I'll sum it up in a few lines: He was born in Austria as a child of the generation who started and lost World War II. His parents, especially his father, instilled a very strong work ethic and a disciplined lifestyle. The German way. Both mental and physical discipline and exercise were present in young Arnold's and his brother's lives. He had to do sit-ups before breakfast, do chores, and play football in the afternoon—competitively. They had to visit other villages and screen plays frequently, and write long essays about these visits for their father. He strictly corrected them. If the kids wanted something, they had to work for it. This type of upbringing instilled in Arnold a deep drive to improve, to achieve, to win—in the beginning, his father's appreciation, and later, much more.

The idea of balancing his body and mind was a key ambition for Schwarzenegger. "You have to build the ultimate physical machine but also the ultimate mind," he tells in his book. "Read Plato! The Greeks started the Olympics, but they also gave us the great philosophers, and you've got to take care of both."[x]

Reading an article about Reg Park, former Mr. Olympia, crystalized the path for Arnold. He decided that the road to America and the road to fulfill his ambitions led through bodybuilding. He bumped into this article by chance by tirelessly seeking the opportunity. Finally, the opportunity found him. Just like I said in the previous chapter—in most cases, opportunity doesn't come as an email offering a CEO job, but as an idea. If you embrace it, with hard work, knowledge, talent, and luck, you can be Arnold. However, to be Arnold, you need to give your life in exchange for these four variables. You have to be all in.

If you feel you have an idea that could change your life and give meaning to it, go for it! Don't be scared of being weird or revolutionary. Don't be afraid to try something new.

Don't collapse under the size of your dream. In fact, it is less risky to aim bigger than to aim mediocre. There's much bigger competition in the middle ground. Doing the unrealistic is easier than doing the realistic. It's quite empty at the top.[xi]

Are you convinced that you can't achieve great things? So is 99% of the rest of the world. Everyone aims for the mediocre goals, so the competition is greatest at that level. Having a mind-blowing goal supplies you with a constant adrenaline rush that gives you the endurance needed to reach it. Mediocre goals, on the other hand, are uninspiring. They won't keep you fueled as much as the big ones, and therefore, sooner rather than later, you'll give it up.

"Don't go where it's crowded. Go where it's empty. Even though it's harder to get there, that's where you belong and where there's less competition."

— Arnold Schwarzenegger

Arnold had clear visions in front of himself. He knew he wanted to be Mr. Olympia, he knew he wanted to move to the US—California. He knew he would break the power lifting record. His visions were so clear that he could almost feel them happening. He had no Plan B, no alternatives; it was that or nothing.

I'm conflicted when it comes to Plan Bs. On one hand, it's a secure way of living; if Plan A doesn't work out, the world isn't falling apart because you still have Plans B and C. Instead of desperation you just take the other ace from your deck. But this doesn't mean that the complete opposite approach to having extra plans can't be just as functional.

Namely, you don't keep a Plan B, like Arnold, but instead concentrate all your might, all your power, time, intelligence, and spirit on your number one goal, Plan A. If you have no alternative, you're less likely to fail since you'll play a game of life and death. If you have more options, you'll likely take Plan A less seriously, and failure is more likely to occur.

This doesn't mean having only one plan is better. It depends on your character.

If you prefer living in a predictable, stable environment, aiming for peace, you should have an alphabet full of plans. Having multiple options will give you security, and almost certainly success— by the rule of large numbers, one should work.

If, however, you're a go-getter overachiever with big dreams, craving to prove yourself, only one goal should be in your focus. The Goal. Parkinson's Law can be applied here. The fewer options you have, the more focused you'll be on that one option. You probably won't be happy and satisfied with anything less than Plan A. Go for it, go all in! Don't go to compete, go to win! Tell yourself, "I deserve that pedestal, I own it, and the sea ought to part for me. Just get out of the f-ing way, I'm on a mission. So just step aside and gimme the trophy." (Arnold Schwarzenegger)

"It's not who you are that keeps you back, it's who you think you're not. So start believing in yourself!"
— Unknown Author

Have Written Goals.

First, put down your ideas on paper and make them very specific. This way you will have "flesh and blood," tangible goals in front of you, not just spirits wandering in the cosmos. What does specific mean in this case? On one hand, what your goal is. On the other hand, when, how, where, and with who you want to achieve it.

For example, let's choose a quantifiable goal. You want to make $100,000. That's the goal.

When do you want it? What's the deadline for it? How do you want to achieve it? Do you need a promotion? Do you want to switch jobs? Pick up a second job? Automate a business to generate passive income?

Where do you want to do it? In your country? Would you move to achieve this goal? Do you see yourself working in an office, remotely?

With who do you want to share this goal? Do you want to have this income as a household? Would you team up with friends or business partners? Do you need the capital, knowledge, or connections of someone to achieve your goal?

Create a mind map along these questions to have a crystal clear idea on what your goal is and what you need to achieve it.

Imagine this process like using Google Maps. It is very different if you only open the app. The map shows up with gray roads. Somewhere in there is your destination. Maybe you'll reach it looking at the uniformly gray roads, guessing which one is the right way. Maybe you'll miss a turn, you'll hit a one-way street, you'll have to turn back, or you'll drift away and might never find your destination. If, however, you put the destination's address into Google Maps, it will show you the shortest, fastest route. It will color it in blue and give you directions. This is the big difference between having clear goals and vague ones.

The Worst Thing You Can Do…

If you want to defeat the impossible, there is a habit you should leave behind quickly. This is worrying.

"If you cannot help worrying, remember that worrying cannot help you, either. Today is the tomorrow you worried about yesterday. If you

worry, you die, if you don't worry you die, so why worry?"

— Unknown Author

Usually, when you step up to fight the impossible, you may hit some roadblocks in the form of worrying friends and family who, at best, question your sanity and the seriousness of your intentions.

"Are you really, really, really sure about this? It's madness. I'd never do this. *It's impossible.*" It's not their fault; they mean well. People who have never taken a big risk in their lives can't understand your aims. Problems and obstacles are all they can see. "But what if something goes wrong?"

In the book *Total Recall*, Arnold shares quite a few personal stories where people, out of disbelief or worry, wanted to convince him that he shouldn't go for what he proposed. His response to them is worth considering.

He told these people that he didn't want to know all the things that could go wrong in his plans. He wanted to walk into the problem first and then ponder the solution, not ahead of time when the issue was not even there.

It's easier to make decisions when you don't know so much about the topic in question. Ignorance about pitfalls can be blissful because you can't overthink them. If you have too much information about the possible obstacles and threats, you might change your mind about trying something challenging.

"Knowing too much is not the answer." Arnold referred to his college economics teacher, who had two PhD degrees and probably knew everything about economics, and still couldn't afford more than public transport to travel.

There is a much bigger chance for success if you stumble onto what you want and deal with the problems when they actually appear. Negative thinking drags your motivation down. What's the worst that can happen if you face a problem? You fail. However, if you don't even give it a try, failure is guaranteed.

"Don't worry about the future. Or worry, but know that worrying is as effective as trying to solve an algebra equation by chewing bubble gum."
— Baz Luhrman

Exercises for This Chapter:

1. Today, I identified three things that I consider impossible but I'd love to do/have/feel/achieve:

1, 2, 3...

_____

2. Today, I wrote down the goal I want to achieve:

3. The precise parameters of this goal are:

What I want to achieve, when I want to achieve it, where I want to go with it, why I want to achieve it, with whom I want to share it...

Chapter 4: On Judgments

"Before you criticize someone, you should walk a mile in their shoes. That way, when you criticize them, you are a mile away from them and you have their shoes."

— Unknown Author

Fear of judgment is one of the key reasons people don't explore their full potential. "What if I'm wrong? What if someone points out that I'm wrong? What if someone is better than I am? What if I end up being a laughingstock?" Familiar thoughts?

People's inner genius might be huge but they never set it free because they avoid making fun of themselves. Understanding the nature of judgment, where it comes from and how it can be controlled, therefore, is especially important to discuss.

Our everyday life is far more influenced by our thoughts about what others think than we realize. On the other hand, we judge others, too. Sometimes we don't even judge consciously. We categorize others into boxes of interesting/boring, pretty/ugly, yes/no without noticing. And others do that, too. It's natural. We will not be everyone's cup of tea just as not everyone will be ours. And that's okay. Our value as humans doesn't decrease because of someone's judgment. And no ones value will decrease because of our judgment.

There is something about judgment that can be actually harmful, though: our blind faith in its accuracy.

Our ability to think and therefore judge sets us apart from other species on the planet. The problem is, we often have blind confidence in our intuition and the accuracy of our assessments. Some of our judgments are far from accurate. Approaching what we know and don't know about others with a little humility can be a game changer.

"Any man who knows all the answers most likely misunderstood the questions."
— Nancy Willard

The information in this chapter isn't aimed at making you lose complete confidence in your judgment. In most cases, you may not be wrong about what you feel on a gut level. The following theories and practices are here to serve as crutches of critical thinking so you can understand and avoid possible errors of judgment.

Nicholas Epley in his book *Mindwise: How We Understand What Others Think, Believe, Feel, and Want* talks about how to reduce the illusion of insight into the minds of others by improving our understanding.

Think about a situation when you had a shortage of information but you had to pick a position on the subject. You constructed a story based on your knowledge and made your judgment accordingly. Maybe you were watching a movie. Halfway through, someone stopped the movie and told you to predict the ending. Let's not take a Nicholas Sparks movie as a basis, where you can predict the ending in the first five minutes. Based on what you saw in the movie up to that moment, you constructed a possible ending.

In real life, we do the same with people. We know some things about them based on our own limited experience or what others told us. Based on these vague pieces of information, we're trying to read the minds of others to make sense of why they act as they do and, of course, to sentence them with our verdict. We can be totally wrong about them. We don't see the whole picture.

Maybe, in the example of the movie, we stopped watching midway through, but in the next five minutes, something crucial would have been discovered that alters your entire perspective on the ending or the character we were judging. We all hated Professor Snape from *Harry Potter*, for example, for being so mean to Harry. We consistently hated him until the series' last installment. I don't want to spoil the reasons, for those who didn't see the movies yet.

We live in "naïve realism." Our intuitive sense tells us that we see the world as it is. It denies that we instead interpret our surroundings as they appear from our perspective. This illusion leads us to believe that we see the world objectively. At the same time, we conclude that others see the world differently. This leads to the conviction that they must be wrong (or biased, ignorant, unreasonable, or stupid). The illusion that we know what we know better than we actually do can make us perceive our minds as being superior to the minds of others.[xii]

A study conducted by researchers showed that the majority of people believe their skills in something are "above average." By definition, above average means better than the average. How can more people be above average than the average?

The answer to this question lies in a glitch in our brains. This glitch is a form of cognitive bias called illusory superiority. We overestimate ourselves in relation to others because we think that we have an empirical advantage that others don't. It's hard to conceptualize that someone from their own perspective has the very same self-righteous sense of self as we do, and from their perspective we are "the other person."

There is no direct antidote to this bias other than awareness. If we acknowledge that we indeed fall prey to this cognitive gullibility and recognize it when we do it, we'll be able to remind ourselves, "Uh-oh, I'm doing this again. I need more information to determine whether or not I'm actually superior in this skill."

The importance of being aware of our own ignorance is something Confucius recognized around 500 BCE.

When Do Judgments Reflect True Knowledge?

Are judgments and predictions more accurate if one has more knowledge about the topic?

Daniel Kahneman, the author of *Thinking Fast and Slow,* is not very optimistic about this correlation.

He showed in his work that people who are considered experts in a particular topic are poor at making predictions, and often are less reliable than the least informed. Why? Because people who acquire more knowledge develop an enhanced illusion of their skills; they become overconfident about their superiority.

In an environment regular enough to be predictable, casual and superficial knowledge isn't enough. Deep knowledge acquired in a changeable environment isn't reliable either. Profound knowledge gained in a stable environment where one can learn the regularities can be considered reliable. When you wish to depend on intuition (others' or your own), first consider whether there was an opportunity to learn enough about the topic—even in a regular environment.[xiii]

This is why I never trust meteorologists 100%. They have more knowledge about weather conditions and predictions than I do, for sure, but nature is so fickle that it's impossible to predict the weather accurately all the time. When I see that it is overcast outside, I put my mini raincoat in my bag just in case. On the other hand, I'd never dare predict the weather, so I still rely more on what the weather forecast says than what I think. I just prepare for possible worst-case scenarios.

This brings us to another variable to consider regarding our objective judgment reliability—how the information is presented. For example, if the weather forecast says it will be 15 degrees Celsius (59 degrees Fahrenheit) and cold, I put on my jacket. However, if they say it will be 15 degrees, nice and warm, I might go out in shorts. Indeed, if I'm primed to experience cold weather, that's what I'll prepare for as a worst-case scenario. If I expect warm weather, my preparations won't be so drastic. We're talking about the weather, but words can sway our perception. So when do I judge 15 degrees Celsius accurately?

Why do I still experience colder or warmer temperature depending on the information I have? It's because my associative memory fell into confirmation bias. In other words, I chose to believe something, so I focus on what confirms this belief. For example, if I believe it is warm outside, I will focus on the sun, the bugs flying around me, how pleasant it is to find a bit of shade, on people wearing thinner clothing, and so on. If I believe it is cold outside, I'll notice the wind and the unpleasantness of the shade. I will look at people who wear thicker clothes, and watch those who are in shorts with bewilderment.

The same happens when someone asks us a question like, "Is this a good place to eat?" Different reasoning will pop into our mind regarding the restaurant's quality than if we had been asked, "Is this a bad place to eat?" Our mind starts searching for confirming evidence, rather than trying to refute. The brain will seek data compatible with the beliefs we currently hold. Even if we don't have the necessary information to form a proper opinion, our mind will jump to a conclusion without asking:

"What would I need to know before I form an opinion about the quality of this restaurant?"

We need a lot of awareness and focus to construct questions like the one above in the heat of the moment. Raising awareness about our confirmation bias-led judgments is key. The more we think about it, the easier it will be to catch ourselves in moments when we do it. Whenever you have to make an important decision, question yourself. Ask, "What is my gut telling me to do? Why? Why do I want to decide this and not the opposite? Am I biased toward this answer?" instead of instinctively jumping to conclusions.

The key message of the book *Thinking Fast and Slow* is that we have two thinking speeds. One is the intuitive, emotional, unconscious, automatic thinking (System 1). The other is the deliberate, rational, conscious, reasoned thinking (System 2). System 1 is the fast, impulsive answer-giver and System 2 is the slow one, responsible for questioning System 1's answers. However, System 2 is lazy and impractical when it comes to fast decision-making.[xiv]

We rarely use slow thinking. We rely on the fast, intuitive thinking instead. We like to trust our intuitions. We are rarely stumped when it comes to answering a question. Instead of questioning our knowledge on the matter, we intuitively form an opinion on the spot.

And in most cases, fast thinking is actually very helpful. How do you put a bag in the rubbish bin? Why would anyone want to think slow about this? Yet the more we introduce slow thinking into our emotionally charged decisions, the better judgments we'll make—we'll be more critical, more objective with our decision-making.

There is another mental glitch I'd like to bring to your awareness. When we are asked a difficult question, we tend to answer an easier one instead.

Our mind subconsciously substitutes the original tough question, "What do I think about it?" with "How do I feel about it?"

But answering the second question isn't the answer to the original question.

This tendency reminds me of my high school years when I had to take oral exams in different subjects. Once I had to talk about the Greek city-states, but I knew nothing about them except pointing out on the map, "This is Sparta!" Instead of answering this question after some generic data, I started talking about how Greek city-states resembled the ones in the Roman Empire, and gradually deflected the topic to the Romans. I knew a lot about that subject. My school-time wickedness illustrates well the difference between the real answer and the answer of a similar but not identical subject.

Try to slow down your thinking deliberately at least five times a day. Ask yourself self-exploratory questions: "Why do I think that?" "Why did I say that?" "Is this really true?" "Is this really the most honest answer I have?"

Being aware of one's own biases and the opportunity to have second thoughts can result in better decision-making, as well as fewer conflicts and misunderstandings.

You can practice slow thinking the following way, "What is my second-favorite flavor?" "What's my third-favorite movie?" Ask yourself questions that require answers other than the obvious. Go beyond the first answer that pops into your mind. Think of two more solutions, and second and third options. Broaden your thinking.

Exercises for This Chapter:

1. Today, I caught myself making up a story about something I knew little about. I even formed an opinion. What questions could I

have asked myself before jumping to that conclusion?

---

2. Based on Kahneman's theory, which are those territories where I have enough knowledge and practical experience in a regular environment to make accurate, intuitive predictions or judgments?

---

3. Today, I caught myself judging based on a stereotype. Now I am taking the time to analyze why I judged based on that. Was I right about it? If I couldn't confirm my judgment, was my judgment fair? What can I do to avoid being prejudicial next time?

Chapter 5: On Time Management

"You get to decide where your time goes. You can either spend it moving forward, or you can spend it putting out fires. You decide. And if you don't decide, others will decide for you."

— Tony Morgan

In conventional thinking, people who are always on time, don't procrastinate (as much), and keep their mind on future goals are considered well balanced and stable. By contrast, people who are living in the past are deemed gloomy, conservative, and stuck. Some belief systems encourage living in the present, moving on from the past, and not stressing about the future.

What is the truth? Is it really better to leave the past behind? Is there any achievement without thinking about the future?

I read a very interesting book on this topic. It is called *The Time Paradox* by Philip Zimbardo and John Boyd. They separated six different time perspectives:

- Past-negative
- Past-positive
- Present-fatalistic
- Present-hedonistic
- Future
- Transcendental-future.[xv]

Each and every one of us thinks in all these time perspectives—some more than others. The authors created a test to find out what percentage of people think in the different time categories.

You can take the test here:

http://www.thetimeparadox.com/surveys/.

At the beginning of this webpage, you'll see a chart with two indicators: "Time Perspective Profile Score Sheet" and "Percentile of People Sharing Your Score." The chart itself shows the optimal amount of "living" in any given time perspective. For example, living in past-negative and present-fatalistic time got the lowest percentage rates, and the past-positive got the highest percentage rate. The optimal time perspective profile is to live high in past-positive, moderately high in future and present-hedonistic, and low in past-negative and present-fatalistic time zones.

To me, this book was a real game-changer. I highly recommend reading it cover to cover. It has such a profound explanation as to why people have different time focuses, and how to shift your time focus when needed.

Why are older people more comfortable with speaking their mind, traveling, or making drastic life changes (like divorcing at 73)? Because they anticipate a limited future. They are not in the "I will never die" mindset anymore. The same mindset applies to those who were diagnosed with a terminal illness. They start working on their bucket list resolutions with more urgency. When you think you have a lot of time, you tend to spend time with a lot of different people. If you anticipate a short future, you value quality over quantity, and spend your time mostly with your loved ones.

Why wait to become old or ill to start living your life to the fullest? Why miss out on the real treasures life has to offer? Acknowledging and changing your time perspectives will truly help you live a better life. What do you think you could improve in your time perspective ratios?

Why Living in the Present is Not Always Rewarding

We need to acknowledge that our time is limited. Just like how birds don't think about their wings as an asset when flying, people don't think about time as an asset either.

Time is the only asset we can't buy, bargain, or trade for any other. It's always running out. Death is our time deadline. I will die—everyone will. (Unless Elon Musk finds the potion of eternal life on Mars.) Living life as if you'll never die means that you think you have unlimited time.

And how do you consider something that is an unlimited resource? Worthless. You don't even think about it. If you feel that something is scarce and you have it for a limited duration, you handle it differently. For example, if you win two hours to drive a Ferrari for free, you'll probably spend every second enjoying the car's power and consider the experience a once-in-a-lifetime one. If you have three Ferraris at home and you win a free ride, you won't even bother to claim your prize. Consider your time as rare, valuable, and scarce as a two-hour Ferrari ride when you've never sat in one.

Denying death has its psychological functions. For instance, it relieves anxiety and stress. However, it may also lead you to live your life less fully and with less value in it. If you choose to live your life with the notion of an unlimited future, your priorities and motivations shift to present satisfactions instead of long-term happiness.

This behavior indicates that you live in the present. As mentioned above, the present can be interpreted in two ways—present-fatalistic and present-hedonistic.

Living in the present, being present, is important for a good life. However, focusing too much on the present can come at the cost of future happiness. Take people who indulge in unhealthy choices without considering their future health.

Undisturbed focus on the future requires political, social, and emotional stability in the present.

People with a present-hedonistic focus are the ultimate enjoyers of the moment. They eat well because they are mentally there when they consume their meal, so they feel the flavors more intensely and have a better experience overall than those who munch through their meal thinking about what they have to do the next day. Present hedonists are the ones who stop to smell the proverbial roses. They seek pleasure and avoid discomfort with the same intensity. They arrange their goals around short-term fulfillment and immediate gratification. They hate routine actions and boring tasks. It is fun and exciting to be around present-hedonistic people because they are generally cheerful, active, and can enjoy life profoundly. They are inspiring with a childlike readiness to connect.

At the same time, they usually have an exaggerated ego, they have trouble controlling their impulses, and they react harshly if something displeases them. They have an unpredictable emotional life.

If present hedonists have enough money, they find great joy in living. They love and appreciate nature, animals, and the people around them. Present-oriented people are more likely to help those in need simply because they notice their problems easily, compared to future-oriented people, who are always in a rush with their mind on the next task, or past-oriented people, who live in the realm of memories. They are less likely to help themselves whatsoever for the same reason. They live in the present. Getting regular health check-ups, buying insurance or floss, and similar preventative precautions are almost nonexistent in their lives.

Zimbardo and Boyd characterize present-fatalistic people as those who focus on this time perspective by nature and not by choice. They are convinced that planning is useless because nothing will work out for them anyway. They don't think they are the masters of their lives; therefore, they often turn to different religions or belief systems that center on a higher controlling power. Others blame the economy, society, politicians, or their fate. Either way, there's nothing they can do about it but accept it. Their lives are mostly pleasure-free, as opposed to present hedonists. Present fatalists are the group most susceptible to depression, behavioral disorders, and suicide attempts out of all the aforementioned time categories. If you get a high score on the time perspective test for present-fatalism, or you can identify with it by reading this summary, take some time to think about why you got this result, how good you feel about your life, and how you could shift to another "time zone."

The benefits of living in the present are cheerfulness, observing the beauty around you, being helpful, living life with high intensity, accumulating many immediate rewards, being optimistic, good and various personal relations, and fearlessness.

The downsides of living in the present are too much carefreeness, being more exposed to illnesses that could have been prevented, unbalanced emotions, higher chance of depression, suicide, and other behavioral disorders, fatalistic mentality, lack of planning, and a lower chance for long-term success.

Why Enhance the Future Time Perspective?

People who are future-oriented are more likely to become successful than those who focus on other time perspectives. They live a less empirical and more abstract planning-oriented life. They put long-term gratification before immediate fulfillment. They are analytical, constantly concerned about the future impact of their present actions. Responsibility, efficiency, and liability are some of the most often used words in their vocabulary. They can work hard and avoid temptations, distractions, and wasting of time to accomplish a goal.

"Failing to plan means planning to fail."
— Brian Tracy

This quote could be the mantra of future-oriented people. They tend to have saving plans and are health-conscious. They are cooperative or competitive, based on which approach results in the highest gains. On the other hand, they have difficulties enjoying the moment since they see it as a waste of time. Every minute, hour, or day spent on pleasures when they could have been productive is wasted.

Compared to present hedonists, future-oriented people have more self-control, consistency, ego control, and seek pleasures less frequently. Compared to present fatalists, they depend less on substances, they are less depressed, have higher self-esteem, and are more energetic.

Future-oriented people live to meet tomorrow's deadline. They couldn't imagine another way of living. They consider their work as a personal mission, and the more success they get as a reward, the more they love working. They look at it as a game. This is why people with future aspirations never stop, never retire, and even if they reach their seven- or eight-figure fortune, they push forward without slowing down. For them, future goals are not about money after a while, but simply about achievement addiction. Unlike present-hedonistic people who live in their bodies, future-oriented people live in their minds. "Emotions deal with the present. Thinking prepares for the future."

Future-oriented folks are the ultimate Type As. They are often absorbed in their work. They seek to get into the flow. They have clear goals, sharp focus, low- or non-existent self-consciousness, and high self-control. People with strong future orientation generally come from financially and emotionally stable families and have a higher education.

People with a transcendental-future mindset are resistant to change, because there is no contradictory evidence for their beliefs. For example, those who strongly believe in God will never change their mind because the inexistence of God can't be proven. When someone tries to contradict their beliefs, they find it insulting, and they become defensive or simply ignore the discussion. Belief in a higher power, heaven, or life after death offers hope and fulfillment in the long-term future. People with transcendental-future aspirations are just as—or even more— active planners and goal-seekers as their regular future-oriented peers. However, their motivations differ. While future-oriented people seek long-term success in this life, transcendental futurists give it all for afterlife rewards.

The benefits of living in the future can be higher chances of success, acknowledging that life is limited and therefore maximizing potential, low time-waste approach, good focus, good analytical skills, improved chances of preventing illness, better financial stability, good planning skills, high self-control, and low self-consciousness.

The downsides of being future-oriented are high levels of anxiety if a deadline is not met, manic behavior, workaholism, existential unfulfillment if their goal isn't satisfying after they achieve it, lack of spontaneity, and they can be controlling in relationships.

The Ups and Downs of Living in the Past

Living in the past always gets a bad rep. However, reliving the past from time to time and focusing on the good memories can help us in our present and give power and hope for a bright future. "How we think and feel today influences how we remember yesterday."[xvi] How we think today also influences our hopes for tomorrow.

The past can be rewritten today; we can give different meaning to past experiences with present optimism. As unbelievable as it sounds, our emotions about past experiences are not set in stone. A research group showed an advertisement to study participants about the amazing things to see and do in Disneyland, including shaking the hand of Bugs Bunny. After the ad was over, people were asked about their own memories. 16% of them clearly remembered being happy for shaking the hand of Bugs Bunny, even though there's no Bugs Bunny in Disneyland. He is a Warner

Brothers character. It is not past events that influence us, but our present perception about them.[xvii]

"To be able to enjoy one's past is to live twice."
— Martial

A healthy amount of nostalgia about past events is rather constructive and helps to boost one's mood. However, extreme focus on the past distracts people from thinking about the future or enjoying the present. Holding grudges and ruminating about negative past events is neither helpful nor healthy.

Positive aspects of a past-focused attitude include a strong sense of self. These people focus on their obligations toward family and community. They are cooperative and they keep traditions alive.

Negative aspects of living in the past: they are noncompetitive; they fear the new, and therefore are not progressive; they tend to be prejudicial and skeptical with improvements and innovative people; they distance themselves from the realities of the present and future; and they tend to feel a strong sense of guilt.

How to Use Time Perspectives to Your Benefit.

People who are lost either in the past or the future, flipping into the present is always a good starting point. The present is the bridge that connects the past to the future. The present is where we experience the happy and hard times.

Do exercises that keep you in the present.

Find out what triggers instant gratification in you, and do it more if you feel that you're too future-oriented. When you start feeling overwhelmed with chasing your deadlines, stop and slow down for a second. Tell yourself, "Stop, stop, stop!" and start doing something that keeps you in the present immediately. Try to find something that you can admire silently around you. Or go and get an ice cream. As health-conscious as you are, you will surely walk it off on the treadmill later. Simply stay in the present for a little while. Do something crazy, something spontaneous, without thinking about the consequences. If you feel you can't do it alone, hang out with a friend who is present-hedonistic.

Observe what thoughts make you sad, depressed, and stuck in the past, and strive to change your thought flow. When you notice yourself thinking about negative things, bring them to your awareness, accept that you just thought about them, and gently let them go. Allow your thoughts to wander somewhere else where you can find joy. Get out of the negative thought spiral. If you feel that you're living in the negative past too deeply, seek out a therapist to help you deal with this problem. Do whatever it takes to decrease past-negative thinking.

Present ties the past and the future into a well-balanced, meaningful continuity. If you're able to look at your time optimally and in a positive light, that's a good sign indicating mental and emotional well-being.

A specific situation always demands the higher presence of a time perspective. Choose the right one for each situation. This means that for a period, one time perspective will emerge while others will stay in the background. For example, when you have career-related challenges and a deadline to meet, flip yourself into a future perspective. When you meet the deadlines, just chill and enjoy the hedonistic moments of the present. When you meet up with old friends and family, be comfortable dwelling in the happy, nostalgic memories of the past.

Each time perspective serves its purpose, and the past-present-future continuum makes life full and provides you with a sense of being.

Exercises for This Chapter:

1. I'm future-oriented by nature. Today, I did this activity to stay in the present:

   _____

2. I'm past-oriented by nature. Today, I did this activity to stay in the present:

   _____

3. I'm present-oriented by nature. Today, I took these steps to get more into the future perspective:

   _____

   a. Today, I took these steps to get more into the past perspective:

   _____

Chapter 6: On Decision-Making

"It is your decisions and not your conditions that determine your destiny."

— Anthony Robbins

Our life is a continuous line of decision-making. Some decisions are easier and some are harder to make. Some decisions we make with such regularity that they become a habit, and our conscious mind doesn't have to be there anymore when we make them. We're on autopilot.

Have you ever stepped out of your workplace and it seemed that you arrived home in no time, but you couldn't recall how you got there? All you did was rumination or future planning on your journey. How was it possible to get home without actively thinking about it? Because you have been on this road so often that your brain memorized it. Nevertheless, this well-known road is still a chain of decisions your subconscious mind makes while your conscious tries to select which muffin recipe to try on the weekend.

Some decisions are not so easy to make, but they are certainly not difficult, either, like what to wear, what to eat, which movie to watch at the theater, and so on.

There are some other types of decisions. The difficult ones, the deal breakers, business, group, family-related decisions that require all our might, all our knowledge, or our spirit to make them.

These decisions often require more than sheer intuition. While you shouldn't ignore what your gut says, a good but hard decision includes more than just your viewpoint. You need to take into consideration different interests. It is not easy to consider all these variables, especially if you're short on time.

This level of decision-making requires individuals to think in systems. Everyone can develop their own system of decision-making with their own parameters. But why do the struggle when so many great decision-making systems have been developed, tried, and proven to work?

I picked a practical, fast, and widely applicable decision-making formula to present in this chapter. This formula can be used from family-related decisions to business negotiations. It is called the Six Thinking Hats™ and was developed by Dr. Edward de Bono. This technique helps you understand a subject from different perspectives using the metaphor of six conceptual hats.

Using this approach, you'll be able to discover and combine the strengths of six different, general viewpoints people usually have. These viewpoints range from optimistic to pessimistic, and rational-positive to emotional-intuitive perspectives.

The six proverbial hats have different colors, and each requires a unique mode of analysis. The six "hats" are the following:

1. The **white hat** stands for information. Focus on the existing, available information only. Make sure to not construct a whole story around the existing elements. Seek out and note the gaps in the knowledge at hand. Look for trends based on the existing information, rather than jumping to conclusions.

2. The **yellow hat** stands for positive thinking. When "wearing the yellow hat," you should be as brightly optimistic as the sun. Consider every constructive aspect regarding your decision. Focus on the optimistic outcome while building confidence and boosting working morale or general motivation.

3. The **red hat** stands for emotions. We are all human beings. Our behavior is not influenced by logic only, but mostly emotional reactions, judgments, suspicions, and intuitions. Taking possible emotional reactions that follow a decision into consideration helps to prepare possible management strategies. Emotions shouldn't be mixed with the objective data whatsoever. They should be handled separately.

4. The **black hat** stands for judgment. While it seems like a bad omen, it is not. Every big decision has weaknesses. There can be flaws, challenges, and hidden risks that should be thought of to preempt them. Better safe than sorry, as they say. Being aware of threats and consciously working on avoiding them is not negative thinking—it is realistic thinking.

5. The **green hat** stands for creativity. This is the hat where people who focus on a future

perspective would thrive. Here you should think abstractly, come up with alternative endings to the situation, and get as creative with each level of the decision making as possible.

6. The **blue hat** stands for overview. This is the part where you think through the entire cognitive process. Look through the ideas and problems found while "wearing the other hats" and identify where they need revision, improvement, or expansion.[xviii]

How Can You Use the Six Thinking Hats™ Technique in Practice?

The topics of the "hats" are given. The main difference in the decision-making process is made by the order of how we use these hats. Let's see an example:

Let's say a clothing company received information that next year's trendy color will be green. Their question is whether or not to go with the flow. They know that almost every competitor will flood its collection with green garments. Should they go for green, too, or differentiate themselves by using the good old marine blue as the dominant color for their collection?

Method 1:

The CEO, creative director, designers, and other employees get together and agree to start the brainstorming session with the BLUE hat and agree upon how the meeting will be conducted. They also define the goal of the discussion: for example, "how to design the collection cost efficiently to be the most marketable for the highest profit." Will they have the green light if they go with the green garments?

When they set the rules, they might move on with the RED hat and discuss subjective and emotional aspects of the question. They flip from being vendors into being customers, and collect ideas about why they, as customers, would choose green garments instead of blue, and vice versa. Everybody voices their subjective opinion on the matter. Some agree that most fashion-conscious people will be influenced by the color trend and will buy the green clothes. Others have a different opinion, stating that most customers are more longevity conscious and know that marine blue is evergreen, while green is just a seasonal color.

When they are done expressing their subjective opinions, they move on to the YELLOW hat, collecting as many positive aspects as possible for both ideas. Pro-green opinions may be the trendy factor, appealing to nature-loving people and people with creamy, darker complexions who like wearing green, etc. For marine blue, they can state that it's a classic color that sophisticated people wear. It's also a business color, so richer businesspeople might choose it as casual business wear. Marine blue can be paired with more colors than green.

Next, the discussion will take place with the GREEN hat on. This is the field of creativity where designers come up with the craziest, coolest ideas to make the products interesting and differentiate them from the rest of the market.

Then comes the WHITE hat and the raw data. The past years' shopping trends, what customers usually buy from their brand, how popular their brand is compared to competitors, production price, etc. They didn't bring data up before because it might have influenced creativity and unbiased thinking.

Lastly, they pick up the BLACK hat and play the devil's advocate, questioning positive ideas, creative ideas, and presenting possible threats and chances of failure.

Eventually, they can put on the BLUE hat again at the end to sum up what has been discussed, and if there are gaps or coherence problems somewhere, fill them. They can also make a final decision, if the provided information significantly tips one side of the scale.

Method 2:

A competitor of the company using Method 1 debates the fate of green clothing with a different approach. They've already made their choice to make a green-dominant collection next year. They want to find the answer to the question, "How do we make our green collection the most sellable?"

They start the debate with the WHITE hat and collect all the facts that can help them. They take into consideration the past year's selling trends, shapes, pricing, average customer's age and gender, and so on.

After that, they discuss each color in a random order: the YELLOW hat for positive ideas, the GREEN hat for creativity, and the BLACK hat for identifying threats.

What they do differently is that they leave a very short (approximately 30 seconds) reaction time for the RED hat, standing for emotions. This way, they'll have time to come up with their very first gut reaction, just like prospective buyers do when they see a product.

They close the session with the BLUE hat summarizing what has been said, highlighting the best ideas, bridging the gaps, and developing strategies to minimize the threats.

Now let's see how you can use the thinking hats in your personal life. If you feel there's no way you can talk a problem through with your partner in a calm, constructive manner, this system can help you a lot. Simply tell your partner that you read about the Six Thinking Hats™ and you'd really like to test it. Summarize to your partner the role of the thinking hats, and present the following discussion order.

You and her can't agree on money matters. You feel that she is not appreciating you enough for the money you spend on her. You'd like to make her understand that you feel taken for granted. Your goal is not to make her pay more; you'd like her to volunteer sometimes for the tab, even if you won't let her pay, or showing some interest in sharing the financial burden.

<u>Method 3</u>:

First, use the BLUE hat and define the problem that needs to be discussed. Agree upon which order to use the hats in through the thinking process.

Since this is an emotional relationship matter, it can't be treated as a raw business decision. It is important to set some rules and agree upon discussion topics at the beginning. For example, make it clear that the black hat—critical thinking—does not equal blaming, so make sure to avoid blaming statements. Make this hat the collection of negative possibilities and outcomes. When the rules are clear and set, switch to the next hat.

This would be the WHITE hat. Both of you collect the facts and relevant information to solve the problem. For example, it is a fact that you pay much more than she does. Her being less powerful

117

financially is also a fact. She never—or very rarely—volunteers to take you out somewhere. Based on these facts, both of you should come up with a few possible logical and neutral solutions.

When you're done discussing the facts, switch to the RED hat and discuss what emotions you feel regarding this issue. You can say that you're not upset about the money, but rather the lack of appreciation and gratitude she shows is what hurts you; that she doesn't say thank you or otherwise acknowledge your weighted contribution.

She might say that she appreciates your financial contribution in a different manner—cooking, washing the dishes, giving you a massage. That's her way of saying thanks. Maybe you didn't interpret her little gestures as such. Make sure to discuss how you express "thank you" and "I love you" in your relationship. Sometimes problems like this are simply a matter of miscommunication.

Brainstorm what the best emotional solution to this problem could be, such as connecting the dinner paid by you to tomorrow's homemade lunch as a sign of appreciation. Or decide to make dinner together at home instead of going out.

Here comes the fang. Put on the BLACK hat and discuss what dangers and consequences may follow if this issue is not treated. You can say that you'll feel more and more unappreciated and may become more irritable, stressed, and distant. She might say that if you make your kindness dependent on money matters and fail to notice her non-financial contributions to the relationship, she might start consider you materialistic and superficial.

Take extra care here not to point fingers at each other. Don't get nasty. Each of you is an individual who has their own value system. Don't debate the reasons why one has those values and issues. Focus on understanding the other party and how to bring these values closer, instead of trying to force the other to change.

When you're done with the dark side, here comes the bright one, the YELLOW hat. Look beyond the pessimistic approach and collect the reasons why you should overcome this problem and make things good for the both of you. The very fact that you can sit down and discuss the issue through the Six Thinking Hats™ is a good indicator that both of you are interested in solving this problem.

When you're in a positive mood full of good expectations, put on the GREEN hat and turn your positive ideas into creative solutions. Set out multiple unique solutions for this matter. For example, she could sometimes offer to pay when the check is not more than 40 dollars. Agree upon how many times you eat out versus how many times you eat at home per week. Set a maximum budget for eating. Try to run away from the restaurant without paying… Just kidding!

Finally, put the BLUE hat on again and summarize what you talked about. If there is anything left to specify or explain, do it. Then, take the best solutions that will satisfy both of you based on the new information you got after the talk.

The Six Thinking Hats™ is an exceptionally efficient and effective multi-dimensional problem-solving and decision-making tool. Using it will save a lot of time by giving you a parallel thinking system, instead of higgledy-piggledy brainstorming. Thinking about an issue through these "hats" will give you enough perspective to make a good to great decision instead of a bad or just okay one.

Exercises for This Chapter:

1. Today, I used the Six Thinking Hats™ technique to make a better business decision:

2. Today, I used the Six Thinking Hats™ technique to solve a relationship issue:

_____

3. Today, I shared my knowledge about the Six Thinking Hats™ technique with this person to help improve their life:

_____

_____

_____

Chapter 7: On Self-Control

"I've learned that everyone wants to live on top of the mountain, but all the happiness and growth occurs while you're climbing it."

— Andy Rooney

When we set a goal, we are very excited about it. We can almost see ourselves victoriously dancing on the top of that proverbial mountain, feeling successful and happy. The dreaming and planning part of each goal is so intoxicating, so attractive. As it should be. If the dreaming and the outcome are not attractive and don't get fired you up, you won't have any motivation to take action.

However, when you start putting the plan into practice to achieve your goal, the happiness, excitement, and a lot of your fuel suddenly disappear. The road to your goal, the implementation of the plan, is not as exciting as the plan itself. You can easily lose spirit when you face the plain reality of the road to success. The vivid, happy picture of achieving your goal will shrink into a small spark. If your goal is not exciting, its fire will completely extinguish.

The road from A to B is plain. It is paved with gray stones and offers less intense emotions than the starting and (perceived) ending points. However, when you reach the end and look back at the road, you'll realize how valuable and meaningful it was.

Achieving a goal is like a car race—competitors are welcomed in the race with loud cheering, limelight, and attractive hostesses. Then they jump into their cars and risk their lives, fighting for glory at a high speed. During the race they won't experience any of the splendor of the beginning. There is only focus, dedication, and challenges.

Even if the race doesn't offer the hedonistic pleasures of the beginning and the end, it offers adrenaline, the chance for improvement and learning, and growth for the better. The race might get boring sometimes, since doing the same lap a couple dozen times is not entertaining, but it must be done to reach the goal.

Focus and willpower keep most people on track to reach their goals. They also have a very clear vision of what they want. What are you focusing on? What are you fighting for?

The reason people don't succeed most of the time is due to the lack of one of these three components: focus, willpower, and clear goal setting. In this book, I've talked about focus and clear goal setting already. Now I will present how you can grow your willpower, why you lose willpower, and how to improve your self-control.

How Do You Improve Self-Control?

To improve your self-control, you have to first self-analyze how and why you lose it. Keeping your actions and emotions under control is crucial to possessing good focus and strong willpower. Remember, passion will be on save mode during your journey to your goal.[xix]

"The road to success is dotted with many tempting parking places."
 — Will Rogers

Collect the distractions that take your control away. Answer the following questions:

> - What are the top three things that distract me all the time, no matter what I do? How can I make sure to prevent these events from happening?

- What are the immediate "wants" that distract me from long-term goal focus?

"To say no when you need to say no, and yes when you need to say yes, you need to remember what you really want."

— Kelly McGonigal

Distractions are bumps in the road that you need to learn how to avoid. You don't have time to change your tires every time you encounter one of them.

Keep your goal close to you—on a sheet of paper, or in the form of a picture or a token that reminds you of what you are fighting for. Always be aware of what you want. The entire world will move out of your way once you know where you are going.

Overcoming immediate "wants" or instant gratifications is especially challenging for those who have their focus on a present-hedonistic time perspective. It can be a good solution to give a name to your impulsive distractions. For example, if you often feel the need to shop for yourself, call the urge "shopaholic schemer." The funny name will help you recognize when the pattern is taking over. Once you are aware of the distraction, you can mindfully say stop and go back to work.

Try to catch yourself earlier and earlier in the process of distraction. Take mental notes on your thoughts and feelings in those moments. Also make a note about the situations that provoke the distractions. (For example, if you work in a café downtown where you have a panoramic view of the mall.) Overcoming instant gratification impulses will require practice and effort. In the beginning, you might fail to control them, but slowly and patiently you'll be able to get this urge under control. Remember—keep your goal in front of you for motivation.

Studies have shown that the human brain is exceptionally responsive to repeated actions. Ask your brain to come up with 10 ideas every day, and it gets better at idea creation. Ask your brain to complicate things, and it gets better at complicating things. Ask your brain to focus, and it gets better at focusing. The more you ask your brain to practice something, the easier it will be to execute the task. If you ask your brain to avoid distractions, sooner or later it will be better at avoiding distractions.

Meditation, for instance, is a great tool to practice self-control. The simple act of staying still, emptying your mind, and not following all your momentary urges makes you better at focusing, managing stress, and self-awareness. People who meditate regularly become much better at self-control in less time.

How do you do meditation? If you can, go in nature, if not, stay inside your favorite room. Focus on your breathing. Inhale. Exhale. Count one when you inhale, two when you exhale. Go on with the counting until you reach ten. Restart. Don't judge yourself if your mind wanders. Just notice the distraction, mentally note "thinking" and gently come back to the breath. Relax your shoulders, your arms, and your legs. Be calm. Do this exercise for at least 10 minutes. At the end, relax your focus and bring your attention back to the room.

Think about the events that challenge your willpower. There is an easy way to escape the challenge: obeying the distraction. But that would mean avoiding success. Imagine yourself going for the harder path. Why do you consider it hard?

Answer this question in your meditative state. Is it the length of the challenge that bothers you? The free time you'd have to sacrifice? Do you have too many "must-do" side activities, like watching TV, binging, or browsing social media that constantly interrupt your flow?

Do you have the answer? Good. Now think about what the inner impulse is that triggers these distractions. What thoughts or feelings lead you to do the distractions you don't want to do?

The next time you feel your distraction coming, keep in mind the following quick solutions suggested by Kelly McGonigal, the author of the book *The Willpower Instinct*, to distract yourself from the distractions.

Slow down instead of speeding up. Slow your breathing to four to six breaths per minute. Count them. Focus on the breathing. Forget about everything else for a little while. Only your breathing matters.

The best mood-boosting, motivation-awakening effects come from short five- to 10-minute intensive exercises. If you feel tired and lacking in motivation, instead of getting lost on social media, do a short, intensive session of jumping jacks. Or do some push-ups. Perhaps go outside for a short walk.

Get enough sleep. When you're tired, your cells don't absorb glucose from the bloodstream as efficiently as when you're well rested. Therefore, they will be under fueled. What will your body do? It will start sending messages to your brain that sugar and caffeine are needed. What do you do? Yes, go and grab your donut and coffee. Distraction mission completed.

Don't wait until you get hungry, either. When your blood sugar drops, your brain turns to short-term thinking, cravings, and impulsive behavior, just like when you were tired. Eat regularly.

Committing to any consistent act of self-control—having breakfast, improving your posture, drinking less coffee, sleeping eight hours, and budgeting—can boost your overall willpower.

The Danger of Moral Licensing.

Sometimes we have the impression that we only self-sabotage if we don't do something well or at all. Yet studies have shown that when we do something good, we can still sabotage ourselves. Why?

When we successfully complete something, we feel good about ourselves. The impact of the positive feedback will lead us to trust our actions. This is not a bad thing by itself—but it can persuade us to let our guards down and give ourselves permission to do something bad.

If you moralize an action you do, it becomes exposed to the effect of moral licensing. For example, if you consider yourself "good" when you eat healthy and "bad" when you eat unhealthy, then the chances are higher that you'll eat fast food tomorrow if you ate salad today. You develop a sense of entitlement for self-indulgence. You feel that you worked for that little piece of chocolate after the gym; it's your reward.

Unfortunately, moral licensing can sabotage your goals big time if you're not conscious about it. When you feel successful, the idea of seeking pleasure doesn't feel wrong. It feels right, you earned it. Without noticing, you'll start acting against your best interests since you are convinced that your self-indulgent behavior is a treat.

You're exposed to the greatest threat if your main motivation for self-control is to become a better person. You might give up and forget your long-term goal as soon as you feel a bit better about yourself.

Did it ever happen to you that while you were working out, you fantasized about what food to eat to make this workout worth the effort? Or did it happen as you lost your first five pounds and you started taking the diet more lightly? Whenever people advance with a goal, many tend to engage in goal-sabotaging activities, mostly by falling back to the good old distraction habits.

Progress can be motivating and trap-free only if you look at your actions as evidence of your commitment toward your aims. You did what you did because you wanted to, not because it was a must. Working toward your goal should feel like the thing you want to do the most, not like a chore. If working for your goal feels like a constant burden, you don't really want that goal.[xx]

When you free yourself from the promise of self-indulging rewards, you'll realize that the reward you were seeking was the main source of your pain. For example, your goal was to lose weight, but after a really good workout you had an ice cream and those pounds didn't move. You became desperate and thought that all was in vain. But when you resisted the sweet temptations, the nasty pounds started flying off.

Eliminating rewards is not the solution. Learn the difference between real rewards that give your life meaning and fake rewards which keep you distracted and hooked. The real reward is to see the day-by-day improvement of your figure, and the professional photoshoot of your dream body in the end. Fake rewards are those five sweet minutes that cost you an extra three-hour workout—which you probably won't do.

Did you know that stress leads to cravings? Negative emotions like anxiety, sadness, and anger push the brain into reward-seeking mode. You want to compensate for your suffering, so you start craving whatever you associate with reward. This can be an activity or a substance; the point is to make you feel better. I, for example, buy stuff much more often when I'm sick, under pressure, or sad.

136

What do you do when you're feeling anxious or stressed?

There are some good anger- and stress-managing activities, like doing physical exercises, attending religious events or praying, meditating or doing yoga, walking, or spending time with your loved ones.

The activities you should avoid to release tension include eating, alcohol consumption, drugs, gambling, computer-related activities (brainless browsing or playing games), and yes, shopping.

Before you give up…

Every one of us hits rock bottom, or has a low point now and then. You can't avoid low points, but you can prepare to handle them in a healthy way. If you're lucky and committed enough to your goal, this low point might knock on your door only once. When it does knock and tempts you to stop, think through the following three statements:

1. If you are tempted to act against your long-term benefit, think about giving up the best possible long-term reward for whatever the immediate gratification is.

2. Visualize that long-term benefit as already yours. Imagine yourself enjoying the fruits of your persistence and hard work.

3. Would you really be willing to give up all that in exchange for a temporary indulgence that is tempting you now?

Keep your eyes on the target. Remember your goal. Remind yourself of whatever your commitment is. If your urges take control, slow down, don't speed up. Listen to your senses. Meditate or walk. Ask your brain to eliminate these urges. Fight them. You can do it. Only you can do it.

Exercises for This Chapter:

1. Today, I committed to do this self-control act consistently to boost my willpower:

_____

2. Today, I released my tension in a constructive and healthy way:

_____

3. Today, I tried to meditate. I could do it for … minutes. Tomorrow's meditation goal is … minutes:

_____

Chapter 8: On Ego

"The ego is only an illusion, but a very influential one. Letting the ego-illusion become your identity can prevent you from knowing your true self. Ego, the false idea of believing that you are what you have or what you do, is a backwards way of assessing and living life."

— Wayne Dyer

What is ego? Ego is one of the biggest obstacles between us and our unlimited self. Ego is arrogance, often a toxic belief in our self-importance. Ego is the devil sitting on one of our shoulders, pushing us to triumph over others, to become more recognized, more famous, richer, smarter.

"Ego is the enemy of what you want and of what you have.

Ego is the enemy of mastering a craft.

Ego is the enemy of real creative insight.

Ego is the enemy of working well with others.

Ego is the enemy of building loyalty and support.

Ego is the enemy of longevity.

Ego is the enemy of repeating and retaining your success."[xxi]

— Ryan Holiday

Our ego very often clouds our judgment. Whenever we achieve something positive, if we're not careful, the ego can capture our mind and boost it to unhealthy heights. We will start to think that "we know it" and that "we're much better than that."

"I know" is the death of growth.

Of course, the opposite also has a negative impact: when we say we don't know anything. The skill to evaluate our abilities objectively, without too much or too little saturation, is a crucial skill to have when it comes to self-improvement. Without it, how can we know if we even improved?

How to Evaluate Your Abilities.

Take a few steps back and observe yourself from a distance. Detach from your self-importance. Think about yourself as one of the many, as a tiny speck of the universe. Realize that you are not as big and important as your ego makes you feel. It sounds diminishing, but if you think about it, this exercise is actually liberating.

The more self-importance you manage to honestly leave behind, the less stressed you'll feel. You'll realize that the everyday matters you momentarily stress about are smaller than a fly's fart. Who cares if your boss said this or that? Or if the grocery didn't have cucumber? Relax.

Stuff doesn't happen to you because of some global conspiracy. Stuff just happens. And while your ego, dwelling in self-importance, stresses about "How could this happen to me—me—me?" you miss the really important things in life. Ego takes away the things that matter—a pleasant afternoon with your kids, a good walk in nature, a loving weekend with your spouse—and replaces them with things that don't—stress, anxiety, and frustration about being the best.

Focus on Actions, Not Words.

Ego is busy with me. What do I want to become? Who do I want to be? What's my purpose on this Earth? These seem like legit questions. Still, they approach the matter from the wrong angle.

What do you want to achieve in life? What accomplishment do you want to leave behind? These questions look for the same answers, but from a non-egoistic point of view. If we achieve something, or accomplish something, it means that others will benefit, too. We think big and act for ourselves, but we also take into consideration the lives of others. The other treasure hidden in these questions is that they are action-oriented. They focus on acting—on "What do I need to do?" instead of "What do I need?"

"Talking and doing fight for the same resources." If you just talk, philosophize, and optimize, you'll never get anything done. You just polish your ego with big ideas, but fail to turn them into reality.

Think big, but humbly execute. Don't aim for something that overwhelms you to the point of idleness. Some dreams sound great, but because you can't truly believe you can execute them, you get trapped in Neverland with your ego. How? The ego is not humble enough to let the idea of the dream go, but it is also not strong enough to start working for it. It traps you in a state where you keep talking and dreaming of the goal, but never savor the real taste of accomplishment.

Learn. Even after You Think You Know.

Lifelong learning is not only good for the brain cells, but also keeps the ego in check. Whenever you commit to learn from someone, you also accept that this person knows more in that domain than you. Admitting the superiority of someone else will temper the ego. Remember, you can't learn if you think you already know.

"As our island of knowledge grows, so does the shore of our ignorance."
— John Archibald Wheeler

Avoid becoming a slave to motivation. Do what you need to do with humility, according to your best knowledge. Chasing motivation puts on you an emotional burden—and a limited time of when you can do work. Motivation slaves are only able to do work when they are "in the zone," or "in the mood." People who think like this hardly ever achieve anything. They will always depend on their mood.

Ego loves motivation. Taking action for a limited time out of motivation is easy. Whatever is beyond it makes the real difference in life. You can start doing something out of motivation or necessity, but to master it you will need more than motivation. It will need hard work and dedication, even in "out of the zone," and "moody" states.

Mastery is a boring, long road filled with learning, failure, and repetition. Does it take 5,000 hours to master something? Nope. There is no finish line.

The ego doesn't want that. It wants the biggest or the finest. It wants to be the biggest, smartest, youngest, "bestest," "firstest"... preferably altogether. All these cravings sentence the lazy man to unhappiness.

Determination, strength, purpose and perseverance will make you grow and improve. Have a goal, have a plan, and then—just do it.[xxii]

Happiness outside Ourselves.

Stay realistic. Remember your purpose. This is something more than a goal. You aim for something greater, something that leaves the boundaries of the self and opts to help others.

Greatness comes from humble beginnings—hands-on work. That is why so many people who become millionaires after being poor are more charitable and have broader purpose than other millionaires. The opposite is also true—a great purpose can humble you.

"The way to do really big things seems to be to start with deceptively small things"—so divide the big chunk into smaller ones. If you stay determined and focused, your purpose won't crumble and you'll eventually fulfill it. Remember, the less you think you are, the more you will do. The more you think you are, the less you'll feel the need to do anything.

Overthinking Thinking.

Some people (their ego) take great pride in their cognitive abilities. They brag about never rushing a decision, thinking everything through—more than twice. People who think all the time end up thinking about nothing but thoughts. This makes them detached as much from reality as from taking action.[xxiii]

General George C. Marshall didn't keep diaries during World War II, even though historians and friends asked him to take notes on his reflections. He didn't want to sacrifice his quiet, meditative time and turn it into some self-indulging performance. He tried to stay away from second-guessing difficult decisions to protect his reputation and polish his image for the sake of future readers.[xxiv]

When you don't know whether or not your ego is controlling you, ask yourself the following question: *What am I missing right now that a more humble person might see?*

The Danger of "Yes."

Many of us have problems saying no, but we are all good at saying yes. Sometimes, we don't even think it through before saying yes to a request—we don't analyze if we'll have time to keep our word. It is easier to say yes to future requests because we don't feel the pressure of the deadline. Sometimes we say yes because we feel interested in something, or we fear to offend the requester.

Other times we say yes because of our ego's insatiable fear of missing out. "Of course I'll say yes to the party, even if I'll die the next day. How could I (the most important person who'll possibly show up) miss it?" Our ego doesn't want to leave undiscovered chances behind. It wants to make sure we present our important self to others. But the majority of these yeses, and the time invested in the execution afterwards, get wasted on superficial things we don't even enjoy, with people we don't like. We waste precious time just to satisfy the ego.

What to do about it? Get a grip on your ego. Ask yourself, "Is this really what I want to do? If this was the last activity I could do in my life, would I go for it?" Discover what path you actually want to walk, and when you have it, stay on track, even when you bump into intersections and forks. Think about what is truly important and leave the rest behind.

It is easier to get off the road once you walk it for a while. You'll start to believe that you now know how to walk it. Moral licensing, remember? You become overconfident and careless—you allow the ego to access your thoughts. It will try to persuade you that now that you're such a good road walker, you should try something else. In other words, it tries to distract you from the good road. Notice this and challenge your ego whenever it wants to sway you. Remember, discomfort is your friend. When you feel it you are on the right track—the ego looks for comfort.

<u>Exercises for This Chapter:</u>

1. Today, I recognized that these decisions were led by my ego:

_____

2. Today, I chose a teacher to learn ......, and thus I defeated my ego:

3. Today, I said "no" to these things to stop feeding my ego:

Final Thoughts

People are not perfect. If your goal is to become the perfect human specimen with an impeccable brain and manners that would shame the British, always making the right decision, seizing the opportunity and managing time excellently, I have bad news.

If your goal is to grow, learn, improve, and expand to become your best self—to reach your "personal excellence"—you will be successful. You have huge potential for self-realization. It is a lifelong road, though; there is no such thing as "no room for improvement."

Try to become 1% better than the day before. Just at one thing—each day, something else. Read five minutes more one day, jog one more block the other day, think before you judge during the third day, and so on. This book has 22 exercises at the end of the chapters. Do one exercise each day for 22 days. They mostly take five to 10 minutes of your life, but they will improve one of your life areas and help you discover more things about yourself. If you don't want to flip back and forth in this book, start doing the idea machine practice—write 10 ideas a day. Try on the thinking hats. Give Pareto's Law a chance and schedule yourself a task with a short deadline and try to meet it.

I hope you got closer to better understanding why you make or don't make certain decisions, steps, and judgments. Train your brain, catch yourself a moment before acting hastily, and enjoy the benefits of becoming a more and more aware YOU.

I believe in you.

Warmly,

Zoe

Before You Go...

How did you like Stretch Your Mind? Would you consider leaving a feedback about your reading experience so other readers could know about it? If you are willing to sacrifice some of your time to do so, there are several options you can do it. Please:

1. Leave a review on Amazon
2. Leave a review on goodreads.com. Here is a link to my profile where you find all of my books.
   https://www.goodreads.com/author/show/1 4967542.Zoe_McKey
3. Send me a private message to zoemckey@gmail.com
4. Tell your friends and family about your reading experience.

Your feedback is very valuable to me to assess if I'm on the good path providing help to you and where do I need to improve. Your feedback is also valuable to other people as they can learn about my work and perhaps give an independent author as myself a chance. I deeply appreciate any kind of feedback you take time to provide me.

Thank you so much for choosing to read my book among the many out there. If you'd like to receive an update once I have a new book, you can subscribe to my newsletter at www.zoemckey.com. You'll get My Daily Routine Makeover cheat sheet and Unbreakable Confidence checklist for FREE. You'll also get occasional book recommendations from other authors I trust and know they deliver good quality books.

Brave Enough

Time to learn how to overcome the feeling of inferiority and achieve success. Brave Enough takes you step by step through the process of understanding the nature of your fears, overcome limiting beliefs and gain confidence with the help of studies, personal stories and actionable exercises at the end of each chapter.

Say goodbye to fear of rejection and inferiority complex once and for all.

Less Mess Less Stress

Don't compromise with your happiness. "Good enough" is not the life you deserve - you deserve the best, and the good news is that you can have it. Learn the surprising truth that it's not by doing more, but less with Less Mess Less Stress.

We know that we own too much, we say yes for too many engagements, and we stick to more than we should. Physical, mental and relationship clutter are daily burdens we have to deal with.

Change your mindset and live a happier life with less.

Minimalist Budget

Minimalist Budget will help you to turn your bloated expenses into a well-toned budget, spending on exactly what you need and nothing else.

This book presents solutions for two major problems in our consumer society: (1) how to downsize your cravings without having to sacrifice the fun stuff, and (2) how to whip your finances into shape and follow a personalized budget.

Rewire Your Habits

Rewire Your Habits discusses which habits one should adopt to make changes in 5 life areas: self-improvement, relationships, money management, health, and free time. The book addresses every goal-setting, habit building challenge in these areas and breaks them down with simplicity and ease.

Tame Your Emotions

Tame Your Emotions is a collection of the most common and painful emotional insecurities and their antidotes. Even the most successful people have fears and self-sabotaging habits. But they also know how to use them to their advantage and keep their fears on a short leash. This is exactly what my book will teach you – using the tactics of experts and research-proven methods.

Emotions can't be eradicated. But they can be controlled.

The Art of Minimalism

The Art of Minimalism will present you 4 minimalist techniques, the bests from around the world, to give you a perspective on how to declutter your house, your mind, and your life in general. Learn how to let go of everything that is not important in your life and find methods that give you a peace of mind and happiness instead.

Keep balance at the edge of minimalism and consumerism.

The Critical Mind

If you want to become a critical, effective, and rational thinker instead of an irrational and snap-judging one, this book is for you. Critical thinking skills strengthen your decision making muscle, speed up your analysis and judgment, and help you spot errors easily.

The Critical Mind offers a thorough introduction to the rules and principles of critical thinking. You will find widely usable and situation-specific advice on how to critically approach your daily life, business, friendships, opinions, and even social media.

The Disciplined Mind

Where you end up in life is determined by a number of times you fall and get up, and how much pain and discomfort you can withstand along the way. The path to an extraordinary accomplishment and a life worth living is not innate talent, but focus, willpower, and disciplined action.

Maximize your brain power and keep in control of your thoughts.

In The Disciplined Mind, you will find unique lessons through which you will learn those essential steps and qualities that are needed to reach your goals easier and faster.

The Mind-Changing Habit of Journaling

Understand where your negative self-image, bad habits, and unhealthy thoughts come from. Know yourself to change yourself. Embrace the life-changing transformation potential of journaling. This book shows you how to use the ultimate self-healing tool of journaling to find your own answers to your most pressing problems, discover your true self and lead a life of growth mindset.

Who You Were Meant To Be

Discover the strengths of your personality and how to use them to make better life choices. In Who You Were Born To Be, you'll learn some of the most influential personality-related studies. Thanks to these studies you'll learn to capitalize on your strengths, and how you can you become the best version of yourself.

Wired For Confidence

Do you feel like you just aren't good enough? End this vicious thought cycle NOW. Wired For Confidence tells you the necessary steps to break out from the pits of low self-esteem, lowered expectations, and lack of assertiveness. Take the first step to creating the life you only dared to dream of.

To access the full list of my books visit this link.

Reference

Books:

Altucher, James. *Choose Yourself.* CreateSpace Independent Publishing Platform. 2013.

De Bono, Edward. *Six Thinking Hats™.* Back Bay Books. 1999.

Epley, Nicholas. *Mindwise.* Penguin. 2014.

Ferriss, Timothy. *The 4-Hour Work Week.* Harmony. 2009.

Holiday, Ryan. *The Ego Is The Enemy.* Portfolio. 2016.

Kahneman, Daniel. *Thinking Fast and Slow.* Penguin. 2011.

McGonigal, Kelly. *The Willpower Instinct.* Avery. 2011.

Newport, Cal. *So Good They Can't Ignore You.* Grand Central Publishing. 2012.

Reh, John F. *Understanding Pareto's Principle—The 80-20 Rule.* The Balance. 2017. https://www.thebalance.com/pareto-s-principle-the-80-20-rule-2275148

Schwarzenegger, Arnold. *Total Recall.* Simon & Schuster. 2013.

Steven Pressfield, Steven. *The War of Art.* Black Irish Entertainment LLC. 2011.

Zimbardo, Philip. Boyd, John. *The Time Paradox.* Atria Books. 2008.

Endnotes

[i] Pressfield, Steven. *The War of Art*. Black Irish Entertainment LLC. 2011.

[ii] Pressfield, Steven. *The War of Art*. Black Irish Entertainment LLC. 2011.

[iii] Newport, Cal. *So Good They Can't Ignore You*. Piaktus. 2016.

[iv] Pressfield, Steven. *The War of Art*. Black Irish Entertainment LLC. 2011.

[v] Altucher, James. *Choose Yourself*. Lioncrest Publishing. 2013.

[vi] Altucher, James. *Choose Yourself*. Lioncrest Publishing. 2013.

[vii] Ferriss, Timothy. *The 4-hour work week*. Harmony. 2009.

[viii] Ferriss, Timothy. *The 4-hour work week*. Harmony. 2009

[ix] Reh, John F. *Understanding Pareto's Principle—The 80-20 Rule*. The Balance. 2017. https://www.thebalance.com/pareto-s-principle-the-80-20-rule-2275148

[x] Schwarzenegger, Arnold. *Total Recall.* Simon & Schuster. 2013.

[xi] Ferriss, Timothy. *The 4-hour work week.* Harmony. 2009.

[xii] Eplay, Nicholas. *Mindwise: How We Understand What Others Think, Believe, Feel, and Want.* Penguin. 2014.

[xiii] Kahneman, Daniel. *Thinking, Fast And Slow.* Farrar, Straus and Giroux. 2013.

[xiv] Kahneman, Daniel. *Thinking, Fast And Slow.* Farrar, Straus and Giroux. 2013.

[xv] Zimbardo, Philip. Boyd, John. *The Time Paradox: The New Psychology of Time That Will Change Your Life.* Atria Books. 2008.

[xvi] Zimbardo, Philip. Boyd, John. *The Time Paradox: The New Psychology of Time That Will Change Your Life.* Atria Books. 2008.

[xvii] Zimbardo, Philip. Boyd, John. *The Time Paradox: The New Psychology of Time That Will Change Your Life.* Atria Books. 2008.

[xviii] De Bono, Edward. *Six Thinking Hats™.* Back Bay Books. 1999.

[xix] McGonigal, Kelly. *The Willpower Instinct.* Avery. 2011.

[xx] McGonigal, Kelly. *The Willpower Instinct.* Avery. 2011.

[xxi] Holiday, Ryan. *The Ego Is The Enemy.* Portfolio. 2016.

[xxii] Holiday, Ryan. *The Ego Is The Enemy*. Portfolio. 2016.

[xxiii] Holiday, Ryan. *The Ego Is The Enemy*. Portfolio. 2016.

[xxiv] Holiday, Ryan. *The Ego Is The Enemy*. Portfolio. 2016.

Made in the USA
Monee, IL
30 April 2021

67307888R00100